The Sabine Series in Literature

T0246600

Series Editor: J. Bruce Fuller

The Sabine Series in Literature highlights work by authors born in or working in Eastern Texas and/or Louisiana. There are no thematic restrictions; TRP seeks the best writing possible by authors from this unique region of the American South.

BOOKS IN THIS SERIES:

Scrap Bones

poems

Library of Congress Cataloging-in-Publication Data

Names: Brown, Collier, author.
Title: Scrap bones : poems / Collier Brown.
Other titles: Sabine series in literature.
Description: First edition. | Huntsville, Texas : TRP: The University Press
   of SHSU, [2023] | Series: The Sabine series in literature
Identifiers: LCCN 2023014066 (print) | LCCN 2023014067 (ebook) | ISBN
   9781680033090 (paperback) | ISBN 9781680033106 (ebook)
Subjects: LCSH: Quality of life--Poetry. | LCGFT: Poetry.
Classification: LCC PS3602.R688 S37 2023 (print) | LCC PS3602.R688
   (ebook) | DDC 811/.6--dc23/eng/20230327
LC record available at https://lccn.loc.gov/2023014066
LC ebook record available at https://lccn.loc.gov/2023014067

Cover design by Miranda Ramírez
Cover Image: "Flow" © Brenton Hamilton
Printed and bound in the United States of America

Published by TRP: The University Press of SHSU
Huntsville, Texas 77341
texasreviewpress.org

Scrap Bones

poems

Collier Brown

The Sabine Series in Literature

TRP: The University Press of SHSU
Huntsville, Texas

TABLE OF CONTENTS

I.

Grind

The Hero's Journey

Clock out. Purple pines
at six p.m. Work was work,
nothing to talk about.
A star looks caught (impaled?)
on the tree I'm peeing under.
When the dog comes round,
he'll know the footprints well.
After all, I'm here a lot:
the hero, just a little drunk,
a little bit depressed,
a little lost sometimes in thought,
just a little bit undressed.

The star in view is not on fire.
Our hero doesn't care if truth is truth
or just a big fat lie. Whichever style
makes music dire, or makes
the dog on scrap bones smile.

Subway Ride

With panic
disorders
like this one,
good luck going
underground.
A metal box
that squeals like slaughter,
no a/c, no windows down
to even imitate
a breeze. I used to think
that chickens, bees,
fresh-air and countryside
might change
the situation—
the ocean, beach,
a cabin in the Alps,
that nineteenth-century
drug on a gentleman's wage.
It's a nice idea,
on the page.
My route to work
is through the Shades,
the Great Shuffling,
the Human Heat.
A guy, strung out
lengthwise
opposite my seat
sings "People Are Strange."
A little on the nose.
Small box of Tic Tacs,
glass tube, socks
arranged across his chest

like artifacts.
He's harmless, I suspect,
though who can say?
Central Station,
now he's a magician,
slips all items up his sleeve.
Once outside,
he warms the glass
with his own breath
and draws a heart,
god knows why,
but good to know
it's not all pain.
I want to stretch out too,
want to dream of what it's like
not so very far,
on a different train.

Autumn & Ativan

I take some consolation in the fact
that even now, I wake before it's time
to be awake, before the sun, before
the lizard has its fill of caddisflies
and the house is like the ocean floor.

Like my grandfather would do—
his mornings never wasted, and every
incremental movement of the clock
a lock undone to doors as large
as Roman arches.
                                    But no, I make
too much of memory. I'm at an age
when urges to reshape the past
like magic take away much more
than what they give. The old man
went to work, sleep-deprived and sore.

And truth be told, probably his lungs
had gathered ash, enough by then
to ache relentless hours. And me?
Because the fear of what it'd mean
to stop this pace wakes me up at three,

I step onto the porch, a coffee
and four Ativan, not nearly middle-
aged. My daughters sleep, and in the haze
of frost and owlet moths: a whiff
of firewood, or someone's house ablaze.

Arrival

I arrive at work
early, not that work
needs doing,
but for the opulent
desolations
of the filing cabinet—
a meager talisman,
but it'll do,
now that years
of stress and panic have
wearied
the single tendon
of my temper.

Nothing picturesque
in view, but far more
preferable: the smell
of stale coffee,
vacuumed carpet,
yellow ledgers, ink.
The quiet here
has nothing wise to say
about its attributes,
and nothing dishonest either,
which is fair
compensation
for the effort made.

This morning
I step into the office
bathroom,
lights off, mopped clean

the night before,
and that cleanness
in the air
a scrubbed lemon zest.
Then the lights.

A cockroach stops
a few feet away,
black like a cavity
on tooth-white tiles.
I know him.
He is the patience
of the river
I grew up on,
2,000 miles south.

There, he's waited
for solitudes
imminent and vast—
he is capable, you see,
of resolutions
worked out in a ferocious
prehuman fire
and floods still to come.
That's why
his appearance
is always out of sync
with human routine,
its clocktime and seasons.
He never truly
arrives, never truly
departs. The quiet

simply shudders
when he flies.

I sidestep.
Long antennae,
like two human hairs,
sway in my direction
which is less a direction
than it is
a ripple in the fabric
that is time,
that is space,
and this is what I mean
by the whole business
of offices at 5 A.M.,
the sleep lost,
the bitter caffeine.
I hurry here
before I start
to forget
that the distances I've crossed
really don't exist.

The Commute

It's late. The commute back home
from work takes longer every week,
though nothing's wrong. My bike's
not broken. The road is just the same.

But it's dark. Well past eight. Along
the road there is a river. An argosy
of geese on the ink-black scene drifts,
asleep. At night, all birds belong

to elsewheres parallel in time,
undisturbed by the nervous sum
of me, plus night, plus stream, plus bike.
Or else, I'm just their dream,

not real, but from a dreamer's view
of men en route to nowhere, true.

The Tetrahedral Kites

i. Alexander Graham Bell & the Preoccupation

By noon, the winds fail. The lull
will mean experiments like this
will have to wait. We'll have our tea
and talk of nothing, just to pass

the time. I'll say, *I know exactly
what you mean*. But I am here
and not here too. I see outside
a shape that's missing from the air

that is my shape, or my misuse
of sight, since nothing like a world
appears. There's just a kite. I mean
for me, there's nothing as controlled

or real. *Dreams*, you say. Yes, and strong.
You think I'm lost. You are not wrong.

ii. Alexander Graham Bell & the Lost Design

When I dream of this, I'm not the age
I am today. We're in our teens.
It's science class. We've made a crate
to keep an egg from spattered scenes

of yolk and shell. You said four sides
can withstand drops from any tower.
What would it have mattered, true
or not, if every unfilled hour

meant an hour more for us? We could
not know that I would still have time
and you, a sum to count by days,
that days would lift us to their rim:

me, in a gift you gave to last
the fall; you, unbroken in the past.

iii. Alexander Graham Bell & His Circle

My friends, watch this. I've taken all
the time I've ever wasted—time
I can't get back, years I've spent
in basements or in books, daydream

or in sleep, hours lost in nowheres,
circumnavigating circles
like all the other rocks around
the sun—and made a kite. Cycles

like the life I lead, and like the ones
you live—let's face it—link themselves
with boredoms far too terrible
to list. And yes, it all revolves

in emptiness, but dignified
when we're together. Watch it glide.

iv. Alexander Graham Bell & the Paper Bird

I'm no good at this. I understand
that motion, any kind, involves
a balance: one left foot to land
where the right foot was. What solves

the problem of the two not going
forward—this is what I mean—
is getting rid of here and now.
So what? you say. *Haven't there been*

a million nows, a million heres?
It's true. I wish I weren't afraid.
But after all, you think we're like
two wings, a paper bird we made

together. If you're right, and we are,
how long can we possibly glide, how far?

No 4 May 10

17

v. Alexander Graham Bell & the Solution

But that's the thing, you think you've got
the end all figured out: what time
you need to spend with X, how much
you need to do for Y. Assume

commitment to the work itself
will be enough to keep disaster
in its cask. For relationships to last,
say B. To pay down debt, master

C. In all of the above, show love
by adding one more job per day.
Swallow H for sleep. For anxiety,
take I. Alone? Depressed? Drink J.

Someday, your kite will reach the air.
If, by then, you even care.

Side View of the Frost King, showing how closely the cells are massed together

Photograph by E. H. Cunningham

19

vi. Alexander Graham Bell & the Winged Boat

After the experiments, the years
spent tying and retying thread
to stones, anchoring your efforts
where you could, awake in bed

all hours, dreaming of a cloud
above a trigonometry
of geese, you think at last, *Enough*.
And here, beneath night's rectory

of stars, dead though they may be
and meaningless and far, and no
keeper of love's paradise, you trade
your kite for a poor man's boat, row

or blindly drift.
                Dear angels, wish
us well, we flightless tribes, we fish.

winged boat with side floats

II.

Cracks

The Expected

The fly in the room is not unexpected.
It's June. Drips of chicken fat warm
like bacterial moors where the sponge
can't get. Crumbs of stale cake across
the edgelands of the floor drive the ants
into a panic. Garbage bags sweat.
The sink's sticky rim ought to be the great
attraction. But the fly in the room's not
preening on the apricot. When it's certain
it can go without, even in the heat
and spoil—that is, when it fastens
to a crease on a fresh, white linen curtain
and waits—you hesitate, but why?
It's not because you're old (you're not)
or that you've given any recent thought
to dying. But something in the way
you step into the frame, ordinary as midday,
rinsed in emollients of plain matter,
hasn't gone unnoticed. Or maybe nerves
are to blame. All the same, something
you have missed, it has not missed.

Anxiety Archives, Entry #738: Zillow

                                                    Collier:
                                        four panic attacks today
                                                        so far
                                            couldn't get on train
                                                 in office now
                                    looking on Zillow for cabins
                                   here's one in VT, 2.5 hr drive
                                         think we cd afford notes?

Candace:
    are you planning on coming home?

                                                    Collier:
                                              it needs a lot
                                                   of things

Candace:
    check out cabin saturday?
    pic looks bad
    needs new roof?

                                                    Collier:
                                              another one
                                           NH, cheaper, 3 hrs

Candace:
    how old?
    says 5 years on market
    what's wrong
    what are you done tonight?
    when

                                                    Collier:
                                       couldn't get on elevator
                                            might sleep in chair
                                                         here

Candace:
oh ok

Collier:
another cabin, how does i look?
it
5 hrs from here

Candace:
You're getting further away

Dragonflies

—Tubing Accident, 1999

I.

Summer kids in the cold lake
keep the dragonflies awake.
The tube is tied behind a boat.

Horseflies swarm a lunatic.
He looks like me. Boat turns
at high speeds, pops us off
our seats. Repeats.

That's the game. We're in the water—
will be in the water, just the same,
now or later. So when the rope
breaks, I'm not surprised.

It snaps a metal chunk of boat
right off, a million miles per hour,
hits me in the face. The dragonflies
are safe. I'm face-down in the water.

II.

Death feels like reprieve. From what?
From what the horseflies cut,
their ounce of flesh, their prize,
their eyes always on our eyes.

Until the yellow, slick tube
flips us into water, the game is bliss
by blistered bliss. Sunburns
and a kiss with teeth, playful
lovely marks, and lakeside fires
after dark, and all the stars that link
to make an archer or a ram.

But where we are is water now,
that's the game, face is down
till someone drags us up
into the boat. We bleed into the lake,
not sure if we're awake.

The dragonflies are dipping for our sake
and ours alone—a glorious green
fire, flashing from each wing.

Somewhere we can hear her sing—
that lady whose last face is pure
darkness in the lake. Now she is awake
and the song tightens light
into a needle-sharp star.

My head hangs over the safety bar
and bleeds into the lake.
My cheek is torn, my teeth
a disappearing trick.

A laceration in the scalp
makes the horseflies lunatic.
The halo they've composed is what
the Christ child's should have shown
in all those manger plays.

I'm bleeding in ten different ways.
Head hangs off the boat. It's
a moment I am trying not to miss,
while the song that makes night
starless keeps singing. And all along,
the blood makes "why" ridiculous.

It's everywhere, it makes a lake.
The dragons fly. For this,
they've stayed awake.

III.

You don't die. The siren-car arrives.
There's urgency, thread to make a scar.
It happens just in time.
For a minute, you were as far as far

can be. Now you're me again. Or
not me again, a different me, a me without
the lake. Even more ridiculous
dragging in your wake that bone-dry

yellow tube, nowhere near lake waters.
Are you so surprised? The dragonfly
still dances for your daughters.
Thank goodness, it goes on.

June heat, elsewhere, still holds
a million-winged green fire
like a snapshot of a lake. The girls are there.
The horseflies bite beneath their hair.

You wonder if they hear, even now,
the Siren as she sings you to distraction.
If they do, it's but a fraction
of the song. Thank goodness for that too.

She sings to the face still bleeding in the lake,
she sings until the light is sharp.
How ridiculous, to miss it,
that starless state. And then the wait.

The Correspondent

It's always back to this: the parts
you see yourself repeat as if
it weren't yourself. *No*, you say
that can't be me: the *I'm okay,*
I'm good, the *Yes, no prob*—my god,
that phony exclamation mark!
So sorry to hear, can I . . . Sure will!
What's he saying now? Again?
Dear X, apologies, I've been . . .
terribly terribly . . . yes, I'm free . . .
No, I could not have said, *Whenever's*
good for you. I could not have written,
Best,

Sparrow Work

Here we are now twenty years
of ours and theirs,
the kids long out of booster chairs.
In fact, they're just as old
as we were
when you told me on the phone,
I can do this on my own—
well, it wasn't TV romance,
was it? Just a way
to be in love as long as love
desires. But then,
we're of that stuff that burns
faster than most fires.
You said *yes* beside
a muddy creek.
We had no dimes, and debt
we had already. I could
not afford a ring, but there
were rings to spare
in the troubled sparrow-wood
that grew around us everywhere.

Remember the tree
outside our trailer?
First home, first ours?
Maples planted artificially
lot by lot, some
semblance of the natural world
in a box where only Hope
(most dangerous)
remains? Sparrows gripped
our branches like a fist.

That ugly, irrelevant bird,
rusty and gray, though in
its divot of dust
happiest. The hurricane felled
the maple closest to us
and broke our home in half.
We gathered all we had
and ran. Our children played.
In the woods,
some hundreds of miles away,
we stood our ground against
downpour, downfall.
Between a million trees
we said, *we're here.*
Conditions being prime
for fear, for death, for hate.
Our third, born in the weeds.
She couldn't wait.
I wish I had better words
for love—words more
lyrical and safe.

All that was long ago—no,
yesterday, right now.
Even when the shades are drawn
at the end of some hard work
of humans at their worst—
ugly and all blade,
uneven as the trees
that will fall down
tonight or in a minute or,
once more, in the final afternoon—

even then, me and you,
never much for wings,
lucky sometimes and unlucky too,
we won't move on,
or haven't yet. After
all this time,
you might or might not
say a word like *love* or stay
another year,
if you could not hear
the trees' awful break.
And on the dirt,
once more, we turn like simple
birds who seem to say
what we had no need to say
above: *Are you okay? Are you*
okay?

Leertretung

—stepping down heavily on a stair
that isn't there (literally, void-stepping)

The Fitbit says a thousand steps
to go. Strike them from the total sum,
a couple hundred million, more
or less. Not counting those at the top
of the stairs, where feet sometimes
step down on nothing, place
having reached its edge, and edge
by the mind outpaced. Thought gone
astray has weight. It adds itself to the skin.
And in its more flirtatious scrapes
with fear, confusion, love, it makes a hole
where no hole should have been.

Nevertheless, the man with no
clue as to why he loves the memory
of sky beyond real sky, photographs
of birds much more than birds, the call
of there better than right here

falls in, breaks a toe, or hits his chin
or worse, never finds his step again.

Orion, Break

Give up the stress
it takes to hold the make-believe
together. Who's the story for?
If for my fathers and my mothers
lost, once, in the desert,
lost once more, in the field,
or once again, dying on the stones,
look now,
they're sleeping in their homes,
they're waking from their beds,
they're at their desks
and on a call. They're unimpressed.
That's not your fault.
Nor your concern. I'm tired
of images, of lines and dots and codes.
When I step into the dark,
I only want the novas
and the nowheres in between,
and if I'm very lucky—
if I've beaten all the odds—
just one, naïve fluoresce
of the insect who
is its own hello/goodbye.

The Fissure

One day he was tired
of the electrical wire
saying too much at once.

His head felt like a dam
with a long, fine fissure
in its weakest wall.

Sickness made its way
into a thought and then
another, laid him on the floor.

Lying there, he asked himself
how far he'd have to walk
to find June's empty fields again.

Just then, the sunlight
slipped a ribbon through
a crack in the front door.
Then a crack in the wall.
Then one more. Then one more.

III.

Elsewhere

More Wreckage in My Home State

—after Hurricane Ida

Ida smashes up the kitchen sink.
Eviction, of a sort, of a kind.

I wonder if the dogs are safe.
Don't tell me they're not chasing
mice and apparitions through wet fern.

When I was boyhood on my else-
where journey, I stood up, wounded,
happy in a flooded ditch.

And there was nothing, nothing,
nothing where the broke-roads crossed
but a way of looking all ways
at once, without aim, without appeal.

I wonder if cicadas bind June days
in stillness, still—those searing bars.

Don't tell me that the nightjars
can't pick, off bricks of heat,
love bugs in their swoons.

I wonder if the dogs have given up
my trace. How quiet
we always were for miles.

I hope the boats will bring them bones
with something still attached.

It's bad enough I don't know who
I am, here in this other place,
nowhere near the post and shrike,
the rust and wire.

Don't tell me that the children
sleep where there's no fire.

Don't tell me the disaster
does not recognize her own.

International Klein Blue (IKB)

To really start this right,
I'd have to steal,
at the very least, two lines
from Larkin's "Church Going,"
but here's some German words
instead: Kaiser-Wilhelm-
Gedächtniskirche, a medieval
church still standing
in Berlin, a hollow tooth,
and by its side, lipstick
and a powder box, all
the stuff you need
to start a Rocky Horror
Picture Show, except,
inside the modern chapel:
walls and walls of blue
stained glass. Blue—
the only word required,
the only word allowable, I think,
to do the grandeur of it justice,
so a moment, if you will,
of genuflection: blue,
blue, blue, blue.
I see it now, again, as it was,
like dropping off
the Mariana Trench
and standing on the bottom,
the only light an awful
blue simmer of swimming
vertebrae, with teeth
to end all happiness.
Even so, I wasn't entirely convinced
that someone locked
in that blue glow
wouldn't (having overcome,

45

if only for a moment,
fear and the fear of fear)
suddenly float an inch or two
upwards. I've known this
feeling once before.
I was mowing baseball fields
alone one summer
in the thick, gluey slaver
of Louisiana's heat.
When lunchtime came,
I ate my Moon Pie
on the pitcher's mound,
watching a distant rain
drop its curtain on the sun
and the day's blue cast
contracting,
its elsewhere so intense,
shattered now and again
by a mosquito swarm,
I felt that to look away
might do some sort of harm.
For this part, I want all
of Larkin's final stanza,
but here's some other words
instead: In 1960, the artist
Yves Klein
created a blue all his own
and rolled nude models
around in it. He also made
a picture of himself
diving out a second story
window. It was not blue.
The works may be unrelated.

Spring in Two Dimensions

—After Gustav Klimt's Rosebushes under the Trees (1905)

When finally the leaflets
leak no light, lapped at each edge,
and the past, the future too,
occupy corners I cannot see—
when the moth's mint wings
dither at the tips of a billion weeds—
when all of it impresses
countless planes of petals, spears,
the third dimension disappears
and somehow darkness with it.
Not a shadow on a spore.

I notice too, there's no room for
intrusion, even if I could
step forward into view. The moon
might beg an audience with such
a spring, but it would have to spare
its reputation, as would anyone
familiar with the night.

The Mask: A Short History

i. Dust Bowl, 1935, New Mexico

When the wall of dust arrives, you want
the dust to *mean*: the angels must have
left us here, moved their guards to the coast,
you think, where the lighthouse
shares its trace with a blue busting up
of surfaces, where the rise of a whale so big,
so much an image out-of-mind, alarms
or mystifies its breathless audience.

Or else it means your turn: four-decade
desert wandering. You might have known
it'd start at the porch. The flies, spit-shined,
clamor to a canine's eye. When the dream
becomes all effort to beget, the insects
you didn't see suddenly distill the view
to what's been there in front of you, even
as you prayed. It's what awaits the sunlight too.

But surely what it cannot mean is that
it *does* not mean. You knot a handkerchief
around your neck and pull the fabric up.
The dust still sediments your pores. At turns,
you mistake yourself for something not yet
born or woken by mistake, dead center of a storm.
You struggle for clean Canaan air, where fruit
in purple clusters wait. Just wait, you think,
it might take years, but the pall will turn itself
to sweetness. It will meet you in green robes
again, do things sane, spill rain for your sake.

ii. Mount St. Helens Eruption, 1980, Washington

And maybe, for a while, it does. The dust,
when sifted through a pleat of curtain sheer,
floats above wide knives of light that cut
the bedroom floor. You think it means much more
because it's art the mind can't make. Of all
the icons dreamed in illness and distraction,
none so simple and not-you confirm despair
as past mistake, and that mistake, the last.
It's all okay, all will be okay.

Then: eruption. And once again, the mask.
You just got here, you think, from all
that wandering. And a stone should take
a billion years to blow break burn. The sense
of it is absent—the doings of a different age,
Vesuvius, the Chicxulub, the boiling seas.

You grab your keys and run out to the street.
You press the cloth against your nose.
Particulates still hot enough to stab steel
blacken out red traffic lights. You might
be in the dark for days, for weeks. Your hand
is in a stranger's hand. No one speaks.
Thin strands of burning hair halo all the city.
In the story, this part should usher in a Judge,
multisighted as a spider. You see the Veil,
the rip of it, the broken vault. But only valves
of waterlines have cracked. Things could
get worse, the dryness long. You grab a pail.

iii. COVID-19, April 2020, Boston

From midnight on to early morning, snow.
It's April. Light is thirteen hours now.
But snow will kill what's taken all this time
to grow. The snow will flake down foot by foot
and make white brine of bluet and the root,
like the truth below Vonnoh's field,
whose lavender and coquelicots—dresses
rinsed in solar flare—were never touched
by pleasure there. Today, the measured low
reads twenty. Rabbits, unpredictably,
tear across the road so fast they go
backwards. Here, not here. Of course, it's not
true, just sentiment, caffeine. I'm no
romantic, just shaken by anxieties too stupid
to explain. I walk the dog. We pass a man, like me,
in a coat and disposable mask. We nod.
Maybe sometime soon, the neighbor's trees
will bud pink in skin-scraped rows. What
an image that will be. What a beautiful mistake.
When it's safe, I lower the mask. Smile
for no good reason. Let the bones show.

In Shinjuku

Finally, I leave him—
that bent nail of an "I"—
back in Boston,
take the plane, put an ocean
and some coastal crag
between the day's long
disrepair and this new me,
drinking Bombay gin
with a stranger in
the other chair.

And then arrive.
Forty million passengers
limn the city
in a quiet script. I see
a ceremony for no one
made of pink crepe
tucked into a wall.
Empty, in this
irresistibly absurd
city of fox shrines and fashion, well,
it's a useless word.

In a crowded alley,
a crow claps against
a black garbage bag.
Another tries to lift
a tattered shoe. It seems
he cannot fly away
without it. *Hello*, I say.
How is it, old friend,
that you've found me here, too?

Brandenburger Tor

In Berlin, a drunk guy's sleeve gets caught
in a subway escalator. He topples, stops
the whole machine, wedged up to his neck.
I tear his shirt, pull him away. His light
goes out. An ambulance breaks the mob.
I've traveled all day, two layovers, a cab,
to find, no, to see, well, maybe just to be
amazed. Now here, I am the scripted ghost
of someone else's movie scene. I look
down at the defibrillator, chest arched up
in a jolt, eyes wide open and empty, or,
suddenly locked with mine. We stare at one
another. He's there and not there too,
the heart not making sense of kilowatts.
Maybe it expected more. He pukes, survives.
I walk away, explore the crowded platz.
A man sells wurst and rice, both sides
of the gate. The pigeons are in paradise.

The Escape

The lizard in my brain,
used to be well trained.

He'd lick his eye, stay still,
bite a moth that wasn't real.

But then the bills, the debt,
the pills, the fear, regret.

And now he's out all day.
He makes himself his prey.

IV.

Fortune

Collier in His Natural State

i. The Color

Obscene candy floss
of Collier's dream.
Try as he might,
Collier cannot seem
to shake the cherries out
this May. Maybe
it's not his fault. Spring's
unembarrassed inks
illustrate the peach's pit.
He almost aches to mention it.
Out of decency, he won't—
ah, but already has. You see
how it unhides
every hidden wish?
It's not just spring.
It's rose year-round.
Except in May it's extra hard
for Collier not to stare
when bees on the field's pink
flush go down.

ii. The Song

Depends on what he's had to drink,
      a singalong, "One Old Brown Shoe."
Depends on dishes in the sink,
      1980s, Mötley Crüe.
Depends on shadows in his brain,
      „Hör' ich das Liedchen klingen"—Fritz.
Depends on vaccines in the vein,
      Phil Collins, all the solo hits.
Depends on work and the workplace lie,
      whistle 'cause that shit is hard.
Depends on dead things in the eye,
      Frank Black y'all, in any chord.
Depends if Collier is alone,
      synthwave and no change of clothes.
Depends on love of the unknown,
      Louis (only) *"La vie en rose."*

iii. The Eye

Collier thinks
he should have been
a sculptor. But
he doesn't have
the skill it takes
to wait. I mean,
the time it takes
to pick from stone
a single lip.
Days? Weeks?
You'd have to fix
his lids with tape.

Voyeur! you say.
Confess,
you're just an eye
without a brain.
Oh yes!
Yes, yes, yes.

iv. The Fool

It'd be a lie, if Collier were to say
he learned to fall in love each day
anew, afresh, again and again,
from gurus in kaupina or soft-skin
Nazarenes in books. His 23-and-Me
gives no further clues. Epiphany
is a plain Wheat Thin. The taste
of a crisp, early a.m. mist
resets some landmine wire
in his chest. Anything can start a fire:
a pencil on an empty desk,
first breath pulling down his mask,
sunspot on the kitchen floor,
dogs running, dogs running more,
white stars on a starling's back.
A list is useless. Good luck,
guessing at the source.
The world gets worse and worse.
Gulf Coast is under mud. West Coast
is burning down. The host
of Collier's country makes
a million ghosts. But Collier wakes
and scrambles eggs, sentimental
about a cup, his crushes accidental,
inappropriate. Even for the moon,
that empty fate, he waits all afternoon.

Thinking like a Seed

Even after forty-one years: a simple thing, still so unexpected. A pinecone on the sidewalk catches my eye. It's closed, gold as butterscotch, and smooth like snakeskin. I pick it up, no big deal, put it by my lamp at work. Two days go by, and here it is, open, all its crisp samaras scattered like tea leaves at the bottom of a fortuneteller's cup. I look it up online: 1.) The water in the cone dissipates. 2.) Its body, tight as-is, contracts a little more, a little more. 3.) So much so, the seeds eject—a life, residual, stored up, cocooned with anticipation known only to itself, leaps toward deadfall and the year's debris. I blow the seeds off my palm from a window on the second floor, watch the little windmills hoist into a dipping breeze. Birds from tomorrow and from yesterday will soon drop down at just the right time, having nowhere else to be.

The Wheel

μῆνιν ἄειδε θεὰ

It was a G.I. Joe, that Hot Wheels trike,
my right and wrong, my four-year-old-
So-Long to naps, plant food, and fear.
Against its jungle green, skinned knees
looked brave. The hot black plastic seat
proved what mettle needed proving.
The sloped driveway was steep, made joy
a downward sentiment. I'd tuck my legs
into my chest and let the wheel adore
its speed, its uncontrolled descent
into the street. At times, I'd fly right off
and bruise, or else I'd cruise into the mud.

No, I don't think life has anything to do
with knowing which side of fortune is which.
And no, I don't expect an equal turn
to come again. There is no dying of
the light, just June and glare, and then no age.
Sing, Collier, make yourself absurd,
ride your wheel into the coming rage.

The Caul

Lastly, nature meets the dock.
S/he's wet, fish slick, or nested, cupped
in tupelo. S/he's tangled up
in moss or glittered on gray mud.
Or else s/he's insect mist, mired
ankle-high by anger. The swarm,
a warmth that's almost human. S/he
is holding blood, at least a smear
of you. And you, of all the river's
children, you should know, the leaves
across the shore, green or gold
or red, they call you for a reason.
They call and call. They call you here.
And not for art, the view, or season.

Starlings

Over Rome,
indecipherable birds
collapse or clone
or bend twilight
into contra-
diction. They have
no idea they're even
here; otherwise, how
could they give
so much of the secret
away, for nothing?

Phyllophaga

The June bug's flown
from god knows where,
and found my bones
unavoidable—
a mistaken acquaintance
with an ancient who,
in this case, is me.
He's been (or she?)
three years underground,
grubbing the sweet
roots. And now
there's only one more year—

no, let's say, 9k more
momentous hours.
It's what I'd like
the trees to think
of my own brief
and fleeting person,
my gratitude
inconsequential
but urgent for
thousands of days.

V.

Yellow

Yarnbombs

I don't have the picture anymore. On a length of cemetery fence, when the trees had already turned rusty and sick, someone had bundled a few twigs with a bit of sunny yellow yarn and tied its loose ends to the wire. It was just hanging there and might have seemed to casual joggersby like nothing but a nest of snagged trash, not uncommon in the city. But someone (someone with red hair and bright green eyes, I imagine) had picked each stick with care, one intrepid leaf still intact, fixed at eye-level like a lanyard.

That was a few years ago, when yarnbombs were a thing. Knitters and non-knitters alike spent weekends at Starbucks darning striped cozies for road signs. In Paris, potholes were heaped with threads all ROYGBIVed. From a distance, they looked like birds of paradise trapped in cracked cement. What a bore museums have become. So predictable, like the church, its fake-flowered lobbies. I think of Uyghur shrines in the deserts of western China, broken branches like teepees, fluttering with scrap cloth and prayer flags, blessed trash heaps, sacrosanct rainbows of debris, and Ireland's wishing trees— their tattered fabrics flapping their wings off the oaks. I've never made a pilgrimage to any holy site. But I saw a lamppost once, socked in the most inviting rouge wool. I stopped my walk to work just to put my finger on it. I always liked the idea of the apostle Thomas—a guy who liked to see dead things get a second chance, a guy with a soft spot for red.

And Now for the Difficult Part

Haven't seen a star
all year. Twelve white deer
part swiftly from a photograph.
They supplement the wild
in the bookstore's Nature
aisle. Prediction: miles more
of snow where June
once captured
in its momentary image
heat with no end, no start.

Always the difficult part:
happiness. Cicadas on
the branch undress.
Keep roses, good, but then
keep weeds. Sparrows
make the hedges sing.
Slip down, friend,
into the lake. We'll dry off
in the smoke, and then
into the bees, follow me.

Two Bumblebees

hover just knee-high
beside my chair.
A drunk June heat undoes
the week's anxiety,
not enough to sleep,
just to stare.
They're lifted, these
two beings, by harmless
vortices of air
(harmless? well, as far
as any life that lives
off life, I suppose)
round and round
the unreachable core.
Off to the side,
my beer has lost its head.
It can wait. I won't
look up to see
a cloud roll or jet roar.
A kindness to the eye
doesn't always make
a clear and obvious shape,
or maybe most days,
it's just too near, too clear.

My Visitor

Dear Accidental Company,
Dear Passerby, Dear Guest,
You might have long caught on
that all that talk of doom was just
presentiments of fall, that Yours Truly
would have to face, late or soon,
that early pearl of autumn moon,
orange acorns root-scattered,
crystal mist when the a.m. comes,
and the lakes all liquid gold.

You might have guessed I'd
take it back: the brooding
and depressed little notes to you
I wrote on black construction pads,
the misanthropic fugues
I shaped like gray balloons
of trash and papier-mâché.

I hope you'll let it pass. Sometimes
I forget what's coming next.
A fox, last night, curled up by the fire
I made of pine blown down by hurricane.
The amber in his hair held the heat
of a wilder sun. You'll never guess
how deep I slept, in that dirt
just a few feet away. You'll never guess.
Guess.

The Apostate

If any man
come to me, and hate
not brother, parent, child,
even his own life . . .

No, not today.
You can keep
Your knife.
What I mean is that
the sun
is yellow as a lemon drop.
My shoes are off,
the grass is soft
as bread. I bought
a peanut butter cup.
It's been eleven hours since
my last anxiety attack.
I do not hate this thing
I'm in, just now.
Where is my child?
Where is my daughter?
Tell her I'm bringing
chocolate.

Spirit

I did it too, sent spit
off to the lab, let strangers
read parts of me
as old as sewing bones
buried in Siberian caves,
and older: old as Sub-
Saharan footpaths—even
old as . . . nevermind—
why try to make sense
of it. Let's just say
it all amounts to an info-
graphic: slight reflux,
eye degeneration,
fourth cousins in Milan,
a smattering of genes
from North Rhine-
Westphalia, and . . .
(let's skip ahead)
a morning off from work,
berries, steel cut oats,
goslings on the lawn
nipping fleas. A line
from *A Time of Gifts*
I can't stop saying aloud,
"moulting eiderdown
of cloud." It's hot outside,
humid, ancient wet.
O Blood, O Memory,
sit here with me a while.
Forget.

Yellow

Man with the Yellow Hat
drinks mojitos at the bar.
Sunshiny yellow jellybean,
him, which is me,
singing all the eighties songs,
singing all the lyrics wrong.

Yesterday I brooded over
bad digestion, prostates,
colons, death, death, death.
I said to myself: "You don't know,
don't sweat it till . . . "
but the voice trailed off
("dying with a dying fall beneath. . .").

The blank, the plank,
the zero. No, no, no,
don't worry yourself, it's in
the math, "conservation (don't
forget!) of energy . . ." I think,
for one brief moment, then
a cool, minty disbelief
and the check, please.

O Consolations, flicker,
flicker! Just a little tune,
like: *Onward particles!*
Outward tiny lightning!
Sing miniscule!

Read Ed Yong's book
last week. So I (???)
am the sum of some
trillion little sprites,
every last one a fan
of David Bowie?
Fair enough. "Dear Life,
w/e're flattered you've
invited u/s . . .
of course w/e'll come . . ."

The party's in the dark,
my Lemon Legion,
Kein Licht! Kein Licht!
Keep the cocktails coming,
turn the music up,
bring y/our panic
close. Let's kiss.

Notes

"The Tetrahedral Kites": Alexander Graham Bell wasn't just interested in transmitting sound over the air. He dreamed of humans taking to the air too. Between 1903 and 1909, he designed and tested enormous kites, strengthened by grids of elegant tetrahedral (pyramid) cells. The journals he kept during this period are illustrated with photographs of Bell and his colleagues, sometimes assembling the kites, sometimes hoisting them upwards, sometimes bracing for disaster. The journals can be viewed on the Library of Congress website.

The photographs inspired my sonnet sequence not because the famous telephone man features in them but because I feel the kite-maker's obsession in myself. We all experience some form of it: the impulse to button our coats, straighten our ties, and set about the doomed business of making something beautiful. I chose the sonnet to match that sentiment and wrote the lines in tetrameter in admiration of Bell's own tetrahedral arrangements.

"Leertretung": an entry from Ben Schott's *Schottenfreude: German Words for the Human Condition* (Blue Rider Press, 2013)

Acknowledgments

"The Tetrahedral Kites" *DIAGRAM* (2021)

"Collier in His Natural State" *The Moth* (2021)

"Starlings" and "And Now for the Difficult Part" *Terrain.org* (2020)

About the Author

Collier Brown is the author of *Eye, Thus Far, Unplucked* (Stephen F. Austin University Press, 2017), *To the Wheatlight of June* (21st Editions, 2013), and *Moth and Bonelight* (21st Editions, 2010). His essays on photography have appeared in over twenty books, and he is the founding editor of *Od Review* (www.odreview.com). Brown teaches at Harvard University.